Oh Susannah:

IT'S IN THE BAG

Oh Susannah:

IT'S IN THE BAG

• • •

The Oh Susannah Series

Carole P. Roman

© 2017 Carole P. Roman All rights reserved.

ISBN-10:1-947118-19-6
ISBN-13:978-1-947118-19-5

Dedicated to all of us who try too hard to be everything to everybody. Remember who is watching.

Teaching kids to count is fine, but teaching them what counts is best.

—Bob Talbert

Special Thanks

To Bianca for all her advice. To Mati for her beautiful illustrations.
Finally, to my Mod Squad Julie, RL, and Alexis.

The five separate fingers are five independent units.
Close them and the fist multiplies in strength.
This is organization.

—James Cash Penney

Contents

ONE	Unfinished Homework	1
TWO	Banana Goes To School	4
THREE	Spiders And Sleepovers	8
FOUR	The Red Pen	11
FIVE	Dogs In Space	13
SIX	The Ripped Zipper	16
SEVEN	Disastrous Dinner	19
EIGHT	Dream Bus	22
NINE	Oh, Susannah	25

CHAPTER ONE

Unfinished Homework

• • •

SUSANNAH WOKE UP IN THE morning. She knew it was early because the sky was a lovely ice blue with a line of pale yellow where the sun was slowly rising over the ridge of the mountaintops. She looked out her window and saw a beautiful star. It was a bright point in the sky, positioned above the highest hill. She held out her hand on the windowsill, measuring the distance of the star with her fingers. It was almost a whole hand span away from the horizon.

Susannah stretched and hopped out of bed. Her unfinished homework was on the floor. She looked at the ten math questions, shrugging. She had answered two of them before she had given up last night. She stared at the raspberry carpet peeking through the tear in the paper. She had erased the answer so hard on the third example that she had rubbed a hole right through the paper. Third grade was proving to be a lot harder than she thought. She peered guiltily around, and then, using her toe, she pushed the homework under her book bag.

Susannah gazed in the mirror. She flared her small nostril to make it look bigger. It made her skin turn pink, clashing with her orange freckles. Her blond hair curled too much to make her happy. She pulled it into a tight ponytail, taming the wild waves.

Her mother called for her to hurry. Mom was always rushing. Between her job and all the things she needed to do every day, her mother never seemed to have much time. Mom sold houses. She was always running to either see a house, take people to see a house or sit with them while they bought the house.

Mom's eyes were constantly on the clock in the kitchen. It was as if their whole life revolved around that big clock. Its ornate oversized hands dictated whether breakfast would be rushed or whether dinner would be meatloaf with a mountain of mashed potatoes or a quick pizza from Phil's.

Susannah could hear its loud ticking, every minute making her mother more frantic. That old clock could determine what kind of day Susannah was going to have, and from the sound of her mother's voice, it was not going to be a good one.

That clock decides a lot in my life, she grumbled to herself. Susannah dressed, not caring if her shirt didn't quite match her pants. Mom yelled again, this time sounding loud and impatient.

Susannah picked up her backpack; the homework lay slightly crushed on the carpeted floor.

"Susannah!" her mother hollered. "I don't have time for this today! I expect you to be down here on time."

Susannah tucked the paper in her backpack between her folders. She eyed the green folder, satisfied the paper was hidden. She was sure no one would see it. Maybe I should show it to my mom; she thought guiltily as she dragged her book bag from the room.

Susannah paused, laying her backpack down on the floor, and reached in to pull out the uncompleted math homework.

I should talk to Mom about it, she murmured to herself.

"Susannah Maya Logan!" Mom sounded harried. "I don't have time!"

Oh, the middle name, Susannah thought. She means business.

Susannah shoved the paper back quickly. "I'm coming," she called as she bounded down the steps.

CHAPTER TWO

Banana Goes To School

• • •

THE KITCHEN WAS A MESS. A box of cereal had been opened, and its contents were strewn across the floor. A bowl of steaming oatmeal waited on the kitchen table. Susannah made a face. She didn't like oatmeal.

Mom was rushing around the kitchen slamming drawers, her shoes crunching on the dry cereal. Her hair was coming out of its neat bun. Mom glanced at that old clock with disgust, grabbed a wet paper towel, and tried to mop up the mess under her feet.

"I wanted Toasty Oats," Susannah complained, her voice whiny.

"I dropped the whole box. Oatmeal is better for you anyway. Don't forget to eat the banana." Her mother was on her knees cleaning up the last of the cereal.

Ugh. Susannah eyed the lump of cooling porridge in her bowl. She glanced at the fruit next to it. She edged it away from her place setting with her knuckle. She hated bananas. Every time she looked at the banana and thought about eating it, the oatmeal tasted like glue in her mouth. She moved the cereal from one side of her bowl to the other.

Mom's back was turned. She was cutting up a snack of carrots to put in Susannah's lunch. Susannah looked longingly at the corn chips in the open cabinet over her mother's head.

Susannah made a face. "Carrots?"

Her mother reached up and shut the door.

Susannah sighed loudly.

"What's the matter?" Mom asked from the kitchen counter.

Susannah stirred her cereal. "Nothing, Mom."

"You sure?" This time her mother looked at her wristwatch. She put the bag of carrots in the brown sack with the rest of Susannah's lunch. Her mother's hands moved quickly—Susannah thought for a minute that must be her superpower. She hadn't quite figured it out yet.

She knew her dad had the ability to see from the back of his head. He always knew what she was doing in the back seat of the car. He attributed this to the eye he said was hidden under his hair. Susannah had looked for it a few times but never found it.

Dad came into the kitchen, throwing a bunch of papers on the table carelessly. He was in a great rush. He leaned over to peck Susannah on her cheek. "I gotta go."

"What?" Her mother turned to see the pile of papers. "You were supposed to do that. I don't know how to fill out those forms. Don't leave them there! They'll get dirty!" she shouted. Mom tossed the brown bag of Susannah's lunch on the table and was hurrying to make a salad for herself.

Her father grabbed Susannah's lunch as he passed by the table.

"You have to do it. It's easy," he called, stopping at the door. He looked at the clock. "I'm late for the train. The deadline for my presentation is today. I can't." He shrugged, stuffing the lunch bag in his cramped briefcase.

Mom looked up. "Wait—that's Susannah's lunch."

"Sorry, honey." He was on his cell phone and out the door.

Susannah watched her lunch leave with her father. She exchanged a sympathetic look with her mother.

Mom opened the cabinet with a little too much force, yanking the peanut butter from the pantry. Her shoulders were hunched together as she spread the peanut butter on the bread, complaining when the bread ripped to shreds. She tossed the first sandwich out and proceeded to make a new one.

Susannah glared at her oatmeal. She wished she had the superpower to make it disappear. It was turning into concrete. She chipped at it with her spoon. She was thinking about her unfinished homework. Maybe now she should tell her mother she hadn't done it. "Mom?" she stated.

Mom threw up her hands. She looked mad. She wiped her palms angrily, stomped over, and shoved Susannah's father's papers into her briefcase, muttering about too much to do and too little time. She looked at the banana on the side of Susannah's plate. Her brows were in a straight line on her forehead.

"Don't forget to eat your banana." Mom looked like she was juggling vegetables at the kitchen counter. She moved rapidly, her eyes on her chore. "I shouldn't have to keep telling you to do that!"

Susannah looked at her mom and then at the banana. Her backpack was propped against her chair. Holding the banana between her thumb and forefinger, she dropped it into her schoolbag behind the folders that hid her unfinished homework. Next went in her remade lunch. She lifted the schoolbag. It wasn't that heavy.

CHAPTER THREE

Spiders And Sleepovers

• • •

Susannah got on the bus and walked to the seat next to her best friend, Lola. Lola was holding an envelope in her hand.

"You didn't take my invitation yesterday." Lola placed it on the seat between them. Susannah didn't pick it up. "You left it on your desk."

Susannah sighed. It was a sleepover for Friday night. Susannah could see the excitement on Lola's face. She knew it was Lola's first sleepover, and her friend couldn't stop talking about it. Lola lived in the oldest house in the neighborhood. It had been built at least a hundred years ago. The last time she visited, Lola's brother, Kai, had talked about the ghost that shared the house. The ghost appeared at night, he had told them. "He drags around heavy chains," Kai had said, holding his hands straight out in front of him. Then he had lurched around the room, groaning. Lola had laughed and said ghosts weren't real, adding, "Wouldn't it be fun to find one?"

Susannah had played in the big old house many times after school. It had lots of narrow hallways and rooms with squeaky floors. Last week, she had gone there to watch a movie with Lola. They had sat together on a huge, comfy couch munching on popcorn. No matter how loud the television was, it couldn't drown out the strange noises filling the house. She heard bangs, squeaks, pops, and cracks.

Susannah had glanced nervously out the living room window. The sun had gone down, and the pale face of the moon made the street look purple. She had looked back at Lola, who was laughing at something in the movie.

The house's floors had creaked; its pipes moaned, making Susannah shiver every time she heard them.

"Doesn't all that noise bother you?" she had asked.

"All old houses are noisy," Lola had told her.

Someone dropped books on the bus floor, and the sound made Susannah jump out of her seat.

"We're going to have so much fun." Lola kept talking. She waved the invitation in front of Susannah's face. "We can stay up all night."

Susannah gulped. Lola had a lot of closets in her bedroom with creaky doors. Susannah stared at the invitation in her hand. It looked big; the paper was thick and heavy. It felt weighted in her hands.

"We can watch another movie. I found a secret door in the basement," Lola told her. "Mom said there's some old stuff down there, and we can look through it!" She squealed with delight.

Susannah gulped again. "But there are spiders in your basement." She wanted to remind Lola about the ghosts but remembered Lola didn't believe in them.

"Spiders!" Lola laughed and waved her hand, dismissing them. "We're gonna have so much fun!"

"Your basement is so dark," Susannah said; her eyes wide.

"Don't worry. I have two flashlights!"

Susannah forced a smile. It felt tight against her lips. Lola looked so happy. She didn't want to disappoint her friend. "Yeah! So much fun!" She unzipped her bag and looked down.

Where could she put it? She took the invitation, carefully sliding it in her schoolbag behind the folders that hid her unfinished homework and under the banana, which looked like it had developed brown freckles.

CHAPTER FOUR

The Red Pen

• • •

Susannah arrived at school, pretending to be excited about Lola's sleepover. Her feet dragged when she walked through the halls. She forgot all about her homework. All she could think about were spiders, creaky floors, and a ghost who dragged around heavy chains. Why did he need the chains? She worried her lip with her teeth. Could this day get any worse? she wondered.

It seemed that it could.

Mrs. Horn had a surprise for the children today. It was a pop-up math test, which surprised Susannah but not in a good way. "I'm expecting you all to know the answers," Mrs. Horn mentioned, her half-moon glasses perched on her nose.

Susannah rested her cheek in her hand and considered the examples. There were ten of them. She recognized them.

They looked like some of the equations in the homework that she hadn't finished. It was tucked behind her folders in her backpack, under her banana, next to Lola's invitation.

The oatmeal felt like a huge lump in her belly. Susannah glanced around the room. Everybody was busy, their number two yellow pencils moving rapidly with the answers.

She tried to do the problems, but in the end, she handed in a paper with a lot of eraser marks.

She took out a workbook to do the next assignment, watching the teacher as she graded the papers. Mostly Mrs. Horn used a blue pen.

Susannah saw her pick up a red pen. She saw Mrs. Horn look at her with her mouth turned down into a frown. Susannah hurriedly lowered her head and continued with her assignment.

Mrs. Horn placed the math test on the corner of Susannah's desk with a big red circle. "I don't know what happened to you today, Susannah. Make sure your mother signs it," Mrs. Horn scolded sternly.

Susannah unzipped her bag, hiding the test between her folders, pressed up against the invitation, behind her unfinished homework, and under the banana that felt a little squishy when she touched it.

CHAPTER FIVE

Dogs In Space

• • •

THE LIBRARY WAS NEXT. SUSANNAH hefted her bag and walked with Lola in the hallway. Her friend chatted happily, ending the conversation when Mrs. Horn told them to be quiet. "Don't forget about Friday," Lola whispered behind her hand.

Susannah took a deep breath, thinking about the invitation in her bag. The straps dug into her shoulder, making her shift the bag uncomfortably. The schoolbag bounced heavily against her back.

"What's wrong?" Lola asked.

"Nothing," Susannah answered.

The library was filled with books on the floor to ceiling shelves. Hundreds and hundreds of books filled the room.

"Did you pick a book?" Lola asked. "I haven't started my report yet."

Susannah shook her head. "Not yet. I can't decide."

The assignment was a week old. Many of the students had chosen their books. Most hurried to their seats to read.

Susannah looked around the room. The shelves looked too high; she couldn't see the titles. Some of the kids were walking up and down the aisles, searching for books to read. Lola was talking to the librarian. The older woman was holding three books. Lola listened intently. Lola paused and picked one. She ran off to start reading it.

Mrs. Austen, the librarian, came over with a new stack of books. "Have trouble choosing a book, Susannah? I have some nice suggestions."

Susannah looked at the stack of books she was holding. Mrs. Austen placed them on the long table. "Well, why don't you consider one of these?" She waited patiently while Susannah considered each one and then added kindly, "Do you need help picking something?"

"No." Susannah shook her head. "I don't need help at all."

Susannah drummed her fingers on the table. There were ten books in front of her. She spread them out. She couldn't decide which to read. She could pick one of the slimmest volumes—that would be the easiest—but none of the stories seemed interesting. One of the thicker ones was about dogs. Susannah liked dogs. There was another about dogs in space. She liked space. She held the two out in front of her.

The cellophane on their covers crinkled noisily. Susannah looked up to see if Mrs. Austen heard the noise.

"Children, make your decisions!" Mrs. Austen called. "Time for gym class."

Susannah glanced at her pile and then at the clock. This clock was smaller than the one at home. Its hands were straight, not curly. They moved from one small minute line to the next. She stared at the face of the clock, the books forgotten on the table. Susannah thought she could hear it ticking too.

Mrs. Austen reminded them this was their last chance to pick a book for the project. Susannah's stomach twisted until it felt like a giant knot was there instead. She kept looking at the books but couldn't decide.

"Which did you chose?" Mrs. Austen approached Susannah with a friendly smile.

The words froze. "Um—dogs," she replied vaguely.

Which book about dogs? Susannah stared at the two books on the table. Mrs. Austen clapped her hands. Susannah felt sweat break out on her forehead. She couldn't make up her mind. A buzzer sounded, making her jump.

She opened her bag, stuffing both books about dogs between her folders, after her unfinished homework, behind the invitation, before the failing math test, and underneath the banana, which started to smell too sweet and looked brown. She lifted the bag. It felt mighty heavy.

CHAPTER SIX

The Ripped Zipper

• • •

GYM PASSED UNEVENTFULLY, EXCEPT THE demerit for forgetting to bring sneakers.

Susannah held up her backpack to Mr. Shore. He looked down at her stuffed schoolbag.

"It's no wonder you forgot them," he said, with a frown. "You don't have room in there. I expect you always to be ready for gym. You know the rules, Susannah." He handed her a pamphlet on the importance of exercising. "Read this with your parents tonight," he ordered.

Susannah held the little booklet in her hand. It was slim. She opened her bag. It was too full. The smell of the banana filled the room. Some of the kids made noises and held their noses. She shoved the fruit aside. She pushed her fingers between the folders in front of the unfinished homework. There was no room.

The tight ball in her stomach was back again. Mr. Shore was watching her intently, his brow furrowed. Susannah made an impatient noise.

The pamphlet was thin enough that she could bend it. She rolled it up and pushed it into her bag, beside the folders, next to the invitation, behind her unfinished homework, in front of her math test, and underneath the now-rotten banana. Then she dropped the books on top of it all.

Susannah tried to pull the zipper closed, but it didn't move. The stuffed bag gaped open like the mouth of a great white shark she'd seen on television during Shark Week. The bag was stuffed. Susannah put it between her feet, squeezing the bag. It stubbornly remained open.

Holding her breath, she tugged the zipper. It moved a little. She could hear the papers inside crackle as they were compressed. Gritting her teeth, she tried to pull the zipper over the small curve of the bag. The over packed bag could not close.

Sighing gustily, Susannah put on her coat and tried closing the bag again. This time she heard a loud *rip*, and the zipper came away from the side of the bag.

The book bag sagged as if the stuffing was knocked out of it. The soft banana had exploded all over the top of her papers.

Lola eyed the bag, her nose wrinkled. "Banana got all over everything?"

"Uh-huh," Susannah agreed; her voice low.

"You want some help cleaning it up?"

Susannah looked at her friend. She didn't want Lola to have to clean up her mess. She didn't want to clean it either.

"I got it. I'll do it when I get home."

Lola smiled and talked the whole way out of the building about the sleepover. She continued chattering the whole ride home and didn't stop until they arrived at Susannah's house.

"See you tomorrow. Don't forget the sleepover!" Lola called.

CHAPTER SEVEN

Disastrous Dinner

• • •

SUSANNAH CAME INTO THE HOUSE. She sniffed the air appreciatively. She smelled food cooking. Maybe it is meatloaf, she thought hopefully. There was the sound of banging pans.

"What's for dinner?" she started to shout as the phone rang. Her mother dropped something big, Susannah ran into the kitchen.

It looked like there had been an explosion of pots in the kitchen. There were pans on the counter and several on the stove. Some looked like they had steam coming out of them. Her mother was dressed in her suit, near her laptop, with a pencil stuck out of her bun. Her jacket was still on, and her briefcase on the floor had papers spilling out of it.

Susannah noticed the papers her father left this morning on the top of the mess.

Mom was talking on the phone. Her cheeks were very red.

"I'll get right on it," she told the other person. "Yes, yes, I'm sorry, but something came up."

Mom caught sight of Susannah. She put her hand over the mouthpiece.

"Go do your homework. I'm busy right now. What..." Her brows lowered when she spoke into the phone. "I said I would take care of it."

Susannah backed out of the kitchen and walked quietly into her bedroom. She dropped her schoolbag on the floor. It landed with a loud thump. Susannah looked at the backpack and then at the door. She could hear her mother shouting on the phone.

The ripped bag seemed so big, as though it took more up than half the room. It was almost as if it was growing bigger. Susannah tried to walk around it, but her foot got caught on the strap. She got on her knees, shoving it toward her bed. It moved slowly. Susannah grunted from the effort, pushing harder. She lifted the dust ruffle and thrust hard. Part of the bag went under the mattress. Susannah turned around, putting her back against the bag. Using her feet, she worked it inch by inch until it fit under the bed.

Susannah straightened the dust ruffle. You can't see my backpack at all, she thought. The doorbell rang, and Mom called for her to come down for dinner.

Susannah ran into the kitchen. There was a pizza box on the table. Her mother's briefcase was on the counter, papers strewn across the surface. There was no steam rising from the pots anymore. The kitchen smelled of wet cardboard and pizza.

"Grab a piece of pizza," Mom commanded. She was holding her phone in one hand, a slice in the other.

"What happened to dinner?" Susannah questioned. Her mom was already in the other room, working on her computer. "Where's Dad?" she said to the empty room.

"He had to work late," Mom yelled. "He has to finish that presentation."

CHAPTER EIGHT

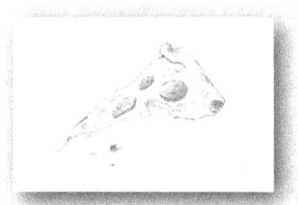

Dream Bus

• • •

Susannah picked at her pizza. Her mind was circling like a hamster in a cage. There was yesterday's homework, the invitation, the math test, the pamphlet, the homework - oh yeah, she thought. I said that one already. The books. She had to choose a book. She watched television, but she couldn't remember what the show was. Susannah got ready for bed. Mom came upstairs.

"Did you do your homework? Brush your teeth? You know what you have to do." Her mother spoke quickly, but Susannah simply nodded. Maybe Mom's superpower was talking fast.

Mom tucked her in bed and turned off the light. She blew a kiss from the doorway. Mom stopped and looked around the room as though something was missing. She opened her mouth to speak, but the phone ringing interrupted her. She glanced at her wristwatch. "Oh," she said. Her brows lowered into a straight line again. They did that when she was worried or angry. "I have to finish. Love you!" she said to Susannah.

Susannah lay flat on her back. The clock next to her bed ticked loudly. She closed her eyes, trying not to hear it, but it kept her awake. She looked out the window. The star had moved over from its spot this morning. She measured its position using her windowsill and three fingers on her left hand. This morning it had taken five fingers. It sparkled in the sky. Her mother used to sing her a song about swinging on a star. Susannah closed her eyes. She pictured herself swinging on a bench suspended from the star. She could feel the cool night air as she drifted back and forth, her mother's gentle voice singing the song.

She shifted uncomfortably, moving her back against the mattress. There was a hard lump digging into her spine. She flopped onto her side. Sniffing, she rubbed her nose and turned over. The smell of ripe banana wafted through the bedding. Susannah covered her face up to her eyes with her fluffy comforter, but the odor sifted through.

She rolled onto her stomach. She was tired. Her eyelids grew heavy. Her breathing slowed, and sound receded. She felt herself relax. She was on the star again, but it transformed into a bus. Lola was holding a flashlight and talking about spiders and ghosts. They bounced on the bumpy road. The bus filled with the sound of clanging. Kai leaned over the seat, his arms outstretched. He was moaning about heavy chains. Susannah glanced at his feet but didn't see any.

The bus grew larger. Something was underneath it, propping it up. It rocked violently. Susannah bent over the side. The schoolbag lay on the ground, expanding under the bus. Susannah was on her knees, holding on with two hands as the bus wobbled. The bus changed into a bed again, and she was alone. Lola and her brother had disappeared.

There was a crunching sound underneath her. She felt it pushing the bed to rise. The bag was pulsing, as if it had a heartbeat, only it sounded like the ticking clock in the kitchen. The noise grew louder. The backpack pushed the bed to the ceiling. The bed teetered from its perch. Susannah's fingers whitened as she gripped the sides. The floor was so far away that she would need a ladder to get down.

The backpack kept growing larger until it took up most of the room. There was a bang, followed by a loud crash. Susannah screamed as the schoolbag exploded, sending papers and bits of banana all over the carpet and walls.

The door opened, spilling light into the room.

"Are you okay", her dad asked, his face worried. He took one look at Susannah and called for her mother.

CHAPTER NINE

Oh, Susannah

• • •

Dad burst into the room, and Mom came rushing in right after him. Susannah was sitting in her bed, rubbing her eyes. She hiccupped and stared at her room in disbelief. Her bed was on the floor. There were no papers or banana in the room—it did smell pretty bad, though.

"What is that smell, Susie?" Mom sniffed the air.

Susannah looked at her parents and put her head down, her cheeks turning red. Her eyes filled with tears. Mom sat on the edge of the bed.

"What's the matter, honey?" Mom moved to the center of the mattress. She bounced on it for a second. "What do you have under here?" she asked.

Susannah slid off the bed and got on her knees. She poked her head under the mattress. She tugged; the broken book bag was stuck. She couldn't get it out. A tear dripped down her cheek. She started to cry louder. Mom joined her on the floor.

Mom repeated, "What is under here?" Mom reached in and tried to get it out. "I can't."

Next, Susannah felt her father move her gently out of the way. "Let me help." He pulled and pulled. The bag was stuck as if rooted to the floor. Dad gave a hard yank, and the bag flew out, emptying half its contents in a banana-smeared mess across her raspberry-colored rug. "Well," he said.

The room was silent except for the ticking of Susannah's alarm clock. Susannah looked at its lighted dial and then at both her parents, who were watching her patiently.

Susannah opened her mouth to tell them, but only a sob came out. Once she started crying, it was as if she couldn't stop. Susannah wailed about invitations, math tests, and book reports, and soon she felt her mother's hands wiping her face.

Her mother sat next to her on the floor. She tugged Susannah into her arms. She rubbed Susannah's back comfortingly. Dad joined them there. Susannah snuggled and wondered for a minute if her mom's superpower was taming crying children.

"Better?" Mom asked.

Susannah gave a slight nod.

"Let's see. This is so heavy!" Mom tried to lift the half-empty bag. She turned it over, spilling everything out. It landed in a great pile. She looked at everything. Susannah's face grew red when she saw her mother pull out the test paper with the red mark. Mom said nothing. Susannah glanced up; her mother's face wasn't mad. Well, it wasn't glad either, but at least her brows weren't across her forehead like a straight line. Dad handed her a tissue, and she wiped the banana off the papers. Everyone was quiet as they considered the lump of papers on the floor.

"This one looks good." Mom held up the book about dogs in space.

A smile tugged at Susannah's lips. "That's what I thought too."

"Are you reading this one for your report?"

Susannah nodded.

"So why are you lugging two books about dogs around?"

"I couldn't make up my mind." Susannah threw her hands into the air, looking at the collection of papers on the floor. "My head feels too full!"

"Oh, Susannah," her father said, sitting on the floor next to her. "Everybody feels that way sometimes."

Susannah looked up at him. "Even you?"

Dad nodded. "Especially me."

They both looked at her mother. "Nobody is superhuman. We all feel that way."

Susannah opened her mouth to ask about the eye in the back of her father's head, but her mother picked up some of the paper, and said, "This isn't so bad. Homework. If you do your homework right away, it doesn't add up."

Dad was looking at the worksheets.

"I couldn't do the homework. I didn't remember how." Susannah whispered.

"I could have helped you." Dad raised his hand as if he were volunteering.

Susannah shook her head. "You had a project, and Mom had a meeting. I hid it in my schoolbag."

"It's overwhelming!" Mom commented.

"What does that mean?"

"Well…" Mom took a moment to think. "Overwhelming means sometimes we have too much of something, and we fall behind in getting things done. This is one big mess."

Susannah repeated the word "overwhelming" slowly, rolling it on her tongue. "Every time I put something in my bag, it felt like it was getting heavier and heavier. Even if it was just a piece of paper!"

"It weighed you down up here." Dad pointed to his head.

"It was too heavy to carry." Susannah sighed. "All I could think about is what I didn't do. It felt like I would never finish."

"I know that feeling." Her mother nodded.

"You do?" Susannah was surprised.

"I sure do. Everybody goes through it one time or another. It's like everything keeps coming at you, and you can't catch your breath. You know what I do?"

Susannah looked up expectantly. "Use your superpowers?"

Mom laughed. "No. I sit back and take a big breath. I stack it all in the middle of my desk and put everything in order of most importance. Then, I go through it one by one. Do you think we can do that?"

Susannah nodded eagerly.

Mom held the pamphlet from gym class. She was reading it, the pages flying. Maybe Mom's superpower was reading fast. Susannah wished she could read as fast as her mother. She hung her head. Her mother's soft hand touched her under the chin.

"Come on, Susannah. We need a solution here. Let's put our heads together and figure this out. How can we make this better? When you look at this large stack, what do you feel?"

"Like I'm choking," Susannah said.

"Susannah." Her father looked up with a gentle smile. "We are always here to help you."

He stood and went to the window. Susannah knew he was still watching her even though he was facing the other way. That secret eye, she thought. She was quiet for a minute. She remembered this morning and then this afternoon when her parents had too much to do. She had to tell them. "You don't make me feel that way," she said simply. "You are always too busy."

Mom's mouth dropped open. Dad turned—his jaw made a big O.

Susannah realized it could go one way or the other. She waited, nervously, her breath caught in the throat.

"You know, I think you're right," Mom agreed finally. "We all put too much pressure on us."

"You keep saying you're expecting," Susannah added in a soft voice.

"What?" Mom and Dad said it at the same time, their voices shocked.

"You do. You expect me to know everything and to do it all right."

"Oh!" Mom smiled. Dad let out a deep breath.

They seemed relieved to have this all out in the open, Susannah thought, feeling a little happier.

"You have a point there, Susie," her father stated. "What can we do to simplify this mess?" He moved to sit on the floor. He gestured at the backpack and its contents.

Susannah stared at the messy stack of papers. She felt the hard knot return to her stomach. It was too much to sort. Her mom had said that she took a deep breath when she felt overwhelmed. Susannah inhaled deeply. She saw her mother smile.

Her parents watched her face. Slowly her mother took one paper, looked at it, and laid it to the side. She picked up another piece of paper and put it next to the first one. Then she took a worksheet and handed it to Susannah. Susannah looked at the assorted piles. She glanced at the page. It was a vocabulary lesson. She placed it on the stack with the English assignments. Next was math; she made a new pile. Susannah watched the mounds grow: spelling in one stack, math in another, and science in the third.

Slowly she put each item in a neat pile. Soon there were four stacks in the room. The backpack looked like a deflated balloon.

Susannah considered the assorted piles of paper. She picked up the one with all her spelling words. "I finished all these."

"Good," her mother said, with a nod. "We can put them in the green folder and move them out of the way."

Dad handed her a folder. Susannah loaded it with the papers and put it to the side.

"What's this?" Mom pointed to the next stack.

Susannah picked up the group of papers. There were four worksheets. She had completed most of the assignments. She looked at each page, noticing she missed two questions. Grabbing a pencil, she put a book underneath the papers to make a hard surface and wrote the answers and looked up expectantly at her mother.

"Looks good to me." Dad was smiling. "Put it in another folder, Susie, and move it out of the way," her father advised.

The next group of papers needed only to be put in order, leaving one last stack. Oddly, Susannah didn't have a knot in her stomach anymore. Four papers left, and she would be done. It didn't feel overwhelming anymore. Susannah smiled with relief.

Her mother looked at her, her head tilted. "Feeling different?"

"Four papers left."

"Only four. You let your work control you, rather than the other way around."

She reached for the neat pile and looked up at her mother with a question in her eyes.

"What does that mean?"

"It means that you have to stay on top of your assignments, and they won't build up."

"I'm not sure how to do this math."

"Try."

Susannah looked at the first example. The clock ticked loudly again. Her eyes traveled to the window, where she watched a plane fly overhead.

"Concentrate, Susannah," her father said softly.

Taking a deep breath, she stared at the numbers. The sounds in the room faded away; she forgot her parents were next to her. The equation started to make sense. In her head, the teacher's instructions replaced the noise of the ticking clock. The next answer came easier. Soon enough, all the examples had neat answers next to them. She looked up to her parents with a smile on her face.

"Good job, Susannah," her mother said proudly.

Susannah sat back. She was thinking how to tell them what she thought. "I'm sorry I didn't do the homework. It wasn't so hard after all. I should have come to you sooner." Susannah stopped for a moment and organized her thoughts. "I think it's okay for you to expect me to know what to do, but sometimes you forget something important too."

"What's that, sweetie?" Mom leaned closer, carefully listening.

Susannah found she could not say the words. She didn't have to talk. Dad held out his arms and embraced his daughter, and said, "I think she's saying that we have to remember she's still a little girl too."

"Not too little," Susannah added.

The phone rang. Mom sighed. She made a move to get up, but Dad stopped her. He said, "Maybe we have to stop expecting too much from everybody in the family and remember what we wanted in the first place."

Mom and Dad took a long minute looking at each other.

"What was that, Dad?" Susannah asked.

"A little girl like you," Dad answered, and the phone stopped ringing.

Mom held up the torn schoolbag with a grin. "Susannah, in your closet is a spare bag, go get it."

Susannah jumped up, ran to the closet, and pulled out a new backpack in a lovely shade of purple. Susannah placed the folders neatly in the backpack.

They worked slowly as if they had all the time in the world. Mom lay down next to her on the bed. Susannah read the first chapter of the book she had brought home, and they learned about Astro the dog's preparation to fly into space. Mom suggested Susannah write one thing she had liked about the book before she went to sleep. After her dad gave her a kiss and left the room, Susannah ended up writing two paragraphs, describing what she enjoyed about Astro's adventure. Susannah looked at her mother, who was watching her with a smile. Her mom had a lot of patience. Maybe patience is her superpower, she wondered.

Mom leaned over to tuck Susannah into bed.

The floor was clean except for an envelope lying half under the bed. Her mother reached for the invitation. "What's this?" she asked.

Susannah took a deep breath, wondering what pile she had for spiders and ghosts. "That," she explained to her mother with a sleepy yawn, "is another story."

www.ingramcontent.com/pod-product-compliance
Lightning Source LLC
Chambersburg PA
CBHW071548080526
44588CB00011B/1831